Fantasy Architecture

Perfect if you love Architecture

Axel Donovan

EVERYTHING IS CANCELLED

GOURMET tapas

廟
安

馬さし
焼肉食べ放題
王道
しゃも
闘鶏
活魚
美加佐
月桂冠
NIWATORI
二和鳥

GOODERHAM & WORTS LIMITED

合格祈願
立命館宇治
中学校
BAHRI
ADE
2020

氷

ROXBURGHE
HOUSE

1744
COACH AND HORSES

CPSIA information can be obtained
at www.ICGtesting.com
Printed in the USA
BVHW091138160822
644713BV00011B/507

9 781803 102351